PENGUIN BOOKS

MY MOBY DICK

William Humphrey is the author of several distinguished novels and collections of stories, including *Home from the Hill, The Ordways, A Time and a Place, Proud Flesh*, and the deeply moving memoir *Farther Off from Heaven*. His hilarious little book *The Spawning Run*, which also explores the life and mores of the dedicated angler, has been called a classic. William Humphrey was born in Clarksville, Texas, and now lives in upstate New York, near a trout stream he will only call Bill's Brook.

BOOKS BY WILLIAM HUMPHREY

The Last Husband and Other Stories
Home from the Hill
The Ordways
A Time and a Place
The Spawning Run
Proud Flesh
Ah, Wilderness! The Frontier in American Literature
Farther Off from Heaven
My Moby Dick

WILLIAM HUMPHREY

MY
MOBY DICK

PENGUIN BOOKS

Penguin Books Ltd, Harmondsworth,
Middlesex, England
Penguin Books, 625 Madison Avenue,
New York, New York 10022, U.S.A.
Penguin Books Australia Ltd, Ringwood,
Victoria, Australia
Penguin Books Canada Limited, 2801 John Street,
Markham, Ontario, Canada L3R 1B4
Penguin Books (N.Z.) Ltd, 182–190 Wairau Road,
Auckland 10, New Zealand

First published in the United States of America by
Doubleday & Company, Inc., 1978
Published in Penguin Books by arrangement with
Doubleday & Company, Inc., 1979

LIBRARY OF CONGRESS CATALOGING IN PUBLICATION DATA
Humphrey, William.
My Moby Dick.
1. Trout fishing. 2. Fly fishing. I. Title.
[SH687.H77 1978] 799.1'7'55 79-9115
ISBN 0 14 00.5271 2

Printed in the United States of America by
The Murray Printing Company, Westford, Massachusetts
Set in Baskerville

TO NICK

MY MOBY DICK

1

CALL ME BILL. SOME YEARS AGO — never mind how long precisely—I thought I would go fishing. It is a way I have of driving away the spleen, and after a winter spent in the Berkshire Mountains of Massachusetts, I had a whale of a swollen spleen. Whenever this happens; whenever I find myself snarling at little children; whenever I stop being grateful that my bottle is half full and start grumbling that it is half empty; whenever I get to thinking of committing myself to a mental institution like the handy one there in Stockbridge— then I account it high time to go fishing as soon as I can, as soon as the season opens—if it ever does. The poet who wrote, "If winter comes, can spring be far behind?" had never spent a winter waiting for spring to come to the Berkshires.

11

Now, when I say I am in the habit of going fishing whenever I begin to grow stir-crazy, I do not mean to have it inferred that I am tormented by an itch for places remote, that I feel the lure of wild and distant seas and mysterious monsters of the deep. Not for me marlin in the Gulf or swordfish off the Patagonian coast. Such fishing costs money, and if I have been saved from evil it is by never having had much of the root of it all. I leave such sport to adventurers who enjoy airplanes and superhighways, motels and roadside franchise food. I never like to journey more than about five miles from home to go fishing, although a reliable report of really good sport can tempt me as far away as ten. When I go fishing I too want to get away from it all, for it is silence and solitude even more than it is fish that I am seeking; but I do not want to have to go far to find it. As for big fish, all is relative. Not every tuna is a trophy. Compared to, say, pickerel, every whale is a whale, but not every whale is a big whale. There are small whales. Every species has its prodigies, and these are not always found where you might expect to find them. While men go in search of them in wild and distant places, it may well be that the monarch of them all lies at this very moment in the shallow waters of that unlikely looking little stream just over the hill behind the house. Tarpon of a hundred pounds are common, and earn their catchers no glory; but Mr. T. S. Hudson got his name in the record book, where it has stood for a generation, by catching a four-and-three-quarter-pound bluegill. To land it must have taken fully five minutes. Which is the pan-fishing equivalent of the three days' battle between Moby Dick and the crew of the *Pequod*.

Now, when I go fishing, I do not hitch a boat to my bumper or clamp a canoe on top of the car and head for the nearest lake. A lake is all too apt to have in and on it other boats, bathers, waterskiers, and for me fishing is an act as private as prayer. Besides, when you've seen one lake you've seen them all, whereas old Heraclitus tells us you can never ascend the same river twice. No boats for me. I do not travel light when I go fishing; I go laden with gear, much of which I seldom use; but a boat is too big a piece of tackle for me. A boat demands so much attention itself, either rowing it or bailing it out, that it interferes with the fishing. The fisherman who fishes from a boat must needs be a boatman, too; me, I am a fisherman pure and simple. To sit in a boat requires patience I have not got. I am sedentary but not that sedentary. I combine hiking with my fishing; when I catch nothing, as is most often the case, I console myself with the thought that I have at least gotten my exercise.

But the principal reason for my dislike of boats is my dislike of impounded water, still water, flat water, silent water, which is to say, stagnant, murky, tepid, weedy, scummy water; nor do I admire the kinds of fish that favor such water. Give me fast-flowing water, cold water, live water, and the fish that thrive in its cold, against its currents. If, in wading it, I sometimes slip on a mossy rock and take a dip myself, I am only the wetter for the experience.

I am particular about my fishing, as you see, requiring that it be cheap, nearby yet uncrowded, in a mountain stream or a meadow brook; and, since it is fishing more than fish that I am out for, I want a fish that will test me — my brains, that is, not my brawn, of which latter I have got even less than of the former. I want a fish that is fastidious and finicky, wily and skitterish, hard to lure, game when hooked. I want one that is not merely edible but delicious, and, while I am at it, one that does not have to be scaled, if you please. "Is that all!" you may say. "Why, the fish you would have must be as rare as white whales—if not as big." I am hard to please; but there is, among all the many kinds of fish that swim, one, just one, that fulfills all my many requirements.

And, that winter in the Berkshires, just over the hill from my house, there was my kind of stream. Frozen hard, still and silent, it was waiting, as I was, for a thaw that was so slow in coming, it seemed that the Ice Age had returned.

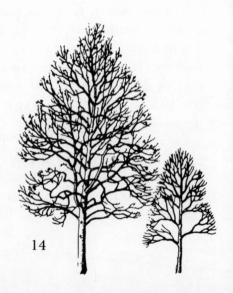

2

I AM NOT ALONE IN MY MONOGAMOUS —even monotheistic—devotion to the trout. There are many fishermen like me—far too many, as far as I am concerned—and I am sure the others all feel that way, too.

What is the appeal of this fish, felt by more men than that of any, perhaps all, other varieties? The trout grows nowhere near as big as the pike, but is there a Pike Unlimited? The trout is not, "pound for pound, and ounce for ounce," as game as the black bass, but who is the black bass's Theodore Gordon, the hermit saint of trout fishing? The catfish provides sport for a greater number of people, yet the best-selling book on fishing of all time, after *The Compleat Angler,* is entitled *Trout,* and rightly so; if you do not agree, whether you be a fisherman or not, try *Catfish.* Whether the trout is the tastiest of freshwater fish is not even to the point, for many fishermen return to the water every one they catch.

I used to think it was the beauty of its habitat that made the trout attractive to fishermen. I thought that until I saw the Beaverkill River in the Catskill Mountains of New York. The Beaverkill is to American trout fishermen what the Ganges is to Hindus. Upon its waters the aforementioned Theodore Gordon floated the first dry fly in the New World—perhaps not quite so momentous an event as its discovery by Columbus, but not far behind that in the estimation of millions of Americans. They said it couldn't be done; that the dry fly, an English invention, was suited only to the placid chalkstreams of England; that upon America's swift, wild mountain streams a dry fly would not float, or would float for so short a time before drag set in (more—much more—on this later) and alerted the fish to the fraud, that it would never work..But, in 1890, Gordon did it. A pilgrimage, once in his lifetime, to the waters upon which this miracle was first wrought, is as obligatory for the American fly fisherman as one to Mecca is for a Moslem.

Let us continue with that comparison. Suppose, reader, that you are a devout Moslem. And that you still have not made your pilgrimage to Mecca, your *hajj*. What though you have prayed facing east five times daily, observed Ramadan, eschewed alcohol, abominated pork, saddled yourself with the prescribed four wives and upon them bred, then brought up a small army of soldiers for the Prophet—all for nought unless you see Mecca before you die. Now suppose that you have scrimped and saved and even borrowed, and you have managed it—just in time, too, for you are not getting any younger. You leave your affairs in other hands and you join the caravan on its long, dusty march. And now suppose that you get there, and you enter the Ka'ba, the holiest of holy places to you, and you find that it has been turned into a pigsty.

I did that. I longed and I planned and I saved, I joined a caravan—it was a traffic jam, actually—and I went to the Beaverkill. And I found that along its banks and spanning its storied pools now runs U.S. 17, a four-lane superhighway that speeds milk trucks and tractor-trailers and mobile homes and traveling sales- men to Binghamton from New York City, and vice- versa.

But the point of my story is this: beneath those overpasses, beside those traffic lanes, indifferent to the din and the rumble and the exhaust fumes, were fishermen—even one fisherwoman. They were not out for meat, but sport of the purest; whatever they caught they were going to have to put back, for there that is the law. It was then that I learned that it is not the beauty and tranquility of its habitat that draws fishermen to the trout. It is the *ding an sich*. To some brothers, and sisters, of the angle, *where* trout live does not mean a thing, so long as they live there. When I cross over the last current of all, I confidently expect to see a certain breed of sinners, oblivious of their burns, casting Rat-faced McDougalls upon the waters of the River Styx.

3

THE HOUSATONIC AT STOCKBRIDGE
inspired Charles Ives to compose a symphony, but to the fisherman I met there
years ago on opening day of trout season, he
on his way up the bank, I on my way down to the water,
it was Shit Creek. "I've heard of it," he said, "and now
I've seen it." He was a fly fisherman, and the sight of
me, with my spinning rod and worm box, was all he
needed to fill his daily limit of disgust.

I am sure the man thought I was too thick-skinned to
feel his barbed look of contempt. If so, he was wrong;
he could not have found another more sensitive to its
sting than I. Wormer though I was, and looking up
from the bottommost rung of the social ladder of angling, I knew its gradations as well as he, who was on top,
did. I had once aspired to climb to the top myself; I had

23

tried and failed. I do not mean to say that I was like the fellow I met while fishing just the other day. He was worming his way downstream, and seeing me ply my delicate art with the tiniest of dry flies (for in the years between the time of the adventures I am relating and the time I am relating them, I have made that climb; what started me climbing again is the subject of this report) said that he had tried fly fishing once— couldn't get the knack of it. I had tried for a whole year. In search of pleasure, I had spent the most frustrating, humiliating and unhappy season of my life, before converting my fly rod into a spinning rod and, thereupon, catching, with a worm, my first trout. But I always felt coarse and inferior, and in the company of my betters I knew my place. Had the man I met on the Housatonic looked more closely he might have seen that mine was as sporting as a spinning outfit could be: a split-bamboo rod weighing just an ounce and a half, a line testing just two pounds. But to him even the most refined worm fisherman was still a worm fisherman, and as Dr. Johnson said, "How does one choose between a louse and a flea?"

As I soon learned, the man was right about the Housatonic, and had the right name for it. The river sounded good and, at a composer's distance from it, looked good—but not at a fisherman's. The worm I dunked in its waters that day did not survive five minutes, and it was not killed by a trout. It was poisoned.

Back at home I found out what had killed the river just by tracing it on the map. Upstream from Stockbridge, the Housatonic flows through Dalton, home of the Crane, the Eaton, and other paper companies. The wastes generated by their mills are—or were then—

discharged untreated into the river. For miles down-stream nothing could live in it.

Herman Melville had another name for the Housatonic, one even more repellent than that fisherman's: Blood River. Melville struck through the mask, the pasteboard mask, and got to the heart of the matter: not the acids generated in the manufacture of the paper, but the life-blood of the millhands—that was the source of the pollution. There can be no doubt that Melville had Dalton and the Housatonic in mind as the setting of his sketch "The Tartarus of Maids," for he himself had recently made the trip he describes in it to Carson's Old Red Mill in Dalton to get "a sleigh-load of paper." He was writing *Moby Dick.*

Melville's strange preoccupation with and horror of whiteness makes yet another appearance in this sketch. On a cold snowy day in January, the narrator, a seed merchant, goes by sleigh to the paper mill to order the envelopes that his business requires by the thousands. His horse is named Black, yet once inside the icy gorge where the mill sits, the horse turns white with frozen sweat. So intense is the cold that the narrator arrives at the mill with frostbitten cheeks, the color all gone from them. His business transacted, he is given a guided tour of the mill. There white rags are shredded by girls as pale as the rags, their lungs ruined by the airborne lint. The rags go into vats where they are turned into a milky mass that reminds the narrator of the whites of soft-boiled eggs. A series of drums rolls the pulp into paper. At the end of the production line another spec-tral woman gathers and stacks the endlessly accumulat-ing sheets of paper. By company rule, the women are all unmarried. This sterility Melville equates with their paleness, the whiteness of the paper they produce (the process takes exactly nine minutes: a gestation period in miniature, resulting in blank sheets) the colorlessness of the wintry scene, the barren setting of the mill. Blood River is like a huge hemorrhage draining away all life from the place, which he calls "The Devil's Dungeon," and leaving all the color of death.

The narrator of the tale—plainly Melville himself in thin disguise—speculates upon the future use of all that paper: "All sorts of writings would be writ upon these now vacant things—sermons, lawyers' briefs, physicians' prescriptions, love-letters, marriage certificates, bills of divorce, registers of births, death-warrants, and so on, without end." It does not occur to him to include the foolscap he himself is writing his sketch on, or the newsprint of the magazine that will publish it. Not to mention the dollar bill he bought the paper with, and those others he was hoping would be spent for that issue of *Harper's Monthly*.

A writer—even one who is a freshwater fisherman—has got to be careful how he curses paper mills.

4

THE ONE OTHER STREAM IN THAT VI-
CINITY was of literary-historical interest
only. A tributary of the Housatonic, this little
creek originated in Stockbridge Bowl, the
big lake below Tanglewood, summer home of the Boston Symphony Orchestra, and meandered down to
Stockbridge, where it joined the river. I rode alongside
it, and at one spot, in the hamlet of Interlaken, four or
five miles downstream, over it, on my way to and from
the library in Lenox, where I went to get the volumes
of Hawthorne and Melville that had been my reading
through that grim, gray winter just past. "Shadow
Brook," the Hawthornes called it, and the dell it runs
through they called "Tanglewood." In the little red
cottage just below today's Tanglewood concert
grounds (or rather, in the original of it, which burned,

and of which this one is a reproduction) the Hawthornes had lived during the year *The House of the Seven Gables* was written. To that cottage, mounted on his saddlehorse and accompanied by his big Newfoundland dog, Melville, himself busy that same year of 1850 writing *Moby Dick,* rode over from Pittsfield to visit, and to tell, in Julian Hawthorne's words, "tremendous tales about the South Sea Islands and the whale fishery," looking, "when the narrative inspiration was on him, like all the things he was describing—savages and sea-captains, the lovely Fayaway in her canoe, or even the terrible Moby Dick himself."

In Tanglewood the Hawthorne children had listened to Eustace Bright—a.k.a. Nathaniel Hawthorne —relate the Greek myths that became *A Wonder Book.* In Stockbridge Bowl and in Shadow Brook Julian Hawthorne learned to fish—an enduring pleasure for him notwithstanding the accident that befell him when, out with his father on the lake one day, their leaky old punt capsized—fortunately, close to shore. Such an ardent fisherman was the boy Julian that he even fished for chickens! Using grains of corn for bait, he fished for them out of the barnloft door. Remembering Shadow Brook more than half a century later, Julian Hawthorne had this to say: "Water, in another guise [other than the lake, he means] dashed and gurgled for us in the brook that penetrated like a happy dream the slumber of the forest that bordered the lake. The wooded declivity through which it went was just enough to keep it ever vocal and animated. Gazing down upon it, it was clear brown, with glancing gleams of interior green, and sparkles diamond white; tiny fishes switched themselves against the current with quivering tails; the shaggy margins were flecked with sunshine, and beautiful with columbines, violets, arbutus and houstonias. Fragments of rock and large pebbles interrupted its flow and deepened its mellow song; above it brooded the twilight of the tall pines and walnuts, responding to its merriment with solemn murmurings. What playfellow is more inexhaustible than such a brook, so full of life, of motion, of sound and color, of variety and constancy?" By my time, well over a century later, it was largely unchanged, and then, too, the fish that switched themselves against its current with quivering tails were still tiny. It was suited, for fishing, for boys only. Indeed, in the section of it that lay in the lower part of Interlaken, the fishing was restricted to children under fourteen.

Boys were fishing in the pool just below the bridge, in upper Interlaken, one day in July when I, on my way home from the library, had a flat there. I watched them from the roadbank as I rested after changing tires. They were catching panfish. But they were neither keeping them nor throwing them back. Whenever a boy landed one he stepped on it to keep from getting finned while he unhooked it. When he had baited his hook again he left the fish to flop on the bank. Very intent they all were, yet no boy bothered to string or even keep track of his catch. Maybe they meant to gather them all together when they had enough and have themselves a fish-fry. They ought to kill them quickly, though, not leave them to flop on the ground until they died.

I was withdrawing my eyes from the scene when they snagged on something. It was something lying in shallow water near the bank downstream from the boys. A

31

log, probably. Or a long, narrow rock. The dappling on it had to be sunlight and shadow. It could not be what it looked like. Not anywhere—least of all in this little roadside puddle. To nobody but a nut on the subject, like me, would any other possibility have occurred.

I got my binoculars from the car. What they showed me was a trout thirty feet long. It could not be included in the glasses' field of view; it had to be scanned, section by section. The spots on it were as big as those on a dappled horse, and gave to it the look of a submarine hull painted in camouflage.

My binoculars being eight power, the fish was actually between three and four feet long. I skipped a breath. I was being shown—I put it that way because I had a strong sense of having been chosen, privileged —one of nature's prodigies, and given a glimpse into her inscrutable ways. Not in the remote, still, unpeopled wildness of Labrador (where it would still have been prodigious) but here in this little roadside pool where cars whizzed at my back and from the houses clustered all around came the mood-music of daytime TV serials, lived one of the world's biggest trout. Few men—I mean by that, say, half a dozen—men, even, whose monomania, whose profession was the pursuit of trophy trout, had ever seen one anywhere near as big. I was of many minds about having been singled out to receive this revelation. I was proud and I was humble. I knew I did not deserve this distinction. I was glad and I was scared. Him whom the gods would bring down, him they first exalt.

Seeing me with my binoculars trained on them, the boys all quit fishing as one and, leaving their fish be-

32

hind, clambered up the bank and fled on their bicycles as though they had been apprehended poaching.

I went down to the water's edge, treading softly so as not to spook the big trout. Some of the bluegills abandoned on the bank were still giving an occasional feeble flounce, others were dead and dry, curled up like shavings; all had had their eyes gouged out. I could account for this barbarity no better after finding a tangle of line with a hook baited with a fish's eye. In addition to being atrocious, it seemed senseless. Catch a fish and pluck out its eyes to catch another fish with, and all only to throw the fish away? This—to say the least—unsporting behavior seemed all the more shocking and saddening in this setting: in the same pool where a truly noble fish lived. One thing I understood: the boys' flight. They knew that what they were doing was wicked.

The big trout lay almost touching the bank. I crept up on him cautiously. I need not have. It was to protect himself where he was unguarded that he lay so close to the bank. His eye on that side, his right, was blind. It was opaque, white, pupilless; it looked like the eye of a baked fish. That, too, was saddening. One hates to see a splendid creature impaired in any way.

An explanation for those boys' behavior now dawned on me. It was pretty farfetched, enough to make me wonder whether I was not a little touched, but I could think of none other to account for the presence together there of the blind fish and the blinded fish. The boys were not fishing for the bluegills, only for their eyes to use as bait. With these they were fishing for the trout. I theorized that they were performing an act of sympathetic magic—or unsympathetic magic, if you will. That they credited the trout with an appetite for, or a hatred of, fishes' eyes because of resentment over the loss of that one of his. I may have been overinfluenced by the literary associations with the place in my mind. I may just have been reading too much Melville. A one-eyed Ahab of trout?

Be that as it may, something that has given me much pleasure, and possibly has kept me out of some mischief, fly fishing, I owe to the two things that came together there at that little pool of Shadow Brook in Interlaken: that big fish and those boys. I was going to fish for the fish, and without reproach to myself that I had trespassed upon the boys' prior claim to him. They had forfeited all right to fish for that trout. It was my revulsion at that ugly business of theirs of gouging out the eyes of living creatures that made me forswear all live—or once live—bait, and determined me to try again, hard as I knew it was, badly as I had been beaten at it before, to learn to fish with artificial flies. Not only that: with dry flies. Nothing but the most sporting of methods was worthy of that once-in-a-lifetime fish. On paper it sounds pretentious, but I felt I had been chosen to atone for those boys and to show that noble trout that not all his human adversaries were ignoble in their ways.

5

T ROUT ARE FISHED FOR AT THREE
DEPTHS: upper, middle, and lower. It is
not immaterial that society, as we know it, is
divided into the same layers. Three families
of artificial flies exist, one for fishing at each of these
depths. They represent the natural insect in three
successive, and ascending, stages of its life cycle. The
complete fly fisherman ought to be adept with all
three, and to know when to use which. In practice it
does not work out that way. A man is drawn to wet-fly
fishing—why is as mysterious as why some men take
up the viola instead of the violin. He becomes a good
wet-fly fisherman, and his loyalty to the wet fly turns
him to it at times when one of the other two kinds
might work better. Another man becomes a good
nymph fisherman; that is the depth at which he likes

to catch fish: when they are feeding on insects after these have left the stream bed and before they have hatched on the surface. He would almost sooner not catch them than catch them in another way. Upon hatching, the insect spreads its wings to dry and rides downstream for a moment before either taking flight or being eaten by a trout. It is this winged stage that the dry fly imitates. The dry-fly fisherman is the most stubbornly loyal of all to his way, and he is the snob of snobs among fishermen. He believes that his way entitles him to the topmost rung of the social ladder of fishing mentioned earlier. The odd thing is, the other kinds of fishermen agree with him on this, and defer to him. They acknowledge him their superior in fishing finesse. On second thought, is that so odd? The assertion of social superiority is usually all that is needed to make others accord it to you. The reason that all other kinds of fishermen look up to the dry-fly purist is not that he catches more fish than they; on the contrary, it is because he catches fewer. His is the sport in its purest, most impractical, least material form.

The wonderful obstinacy of the dry-fly purist! The odds which he knows are against him, and despite this—or because of it—his pertinacity, his lofty indifference to mere gross success, his concentration upon means, not ends! Let him be on public water, water without restrictions as to tackle and baits. Along comes a worm fisherman, his creel heavy with fish. The dry-fly man not only does not envy him his catch, he despises the oaf. Along comes a spin fisherman, one whose outfit allows him to fish bushy places where the fly fisherman cannot penetrate, and who, with his metal lures, has taken his limit. "Hardware merchant," is the dry-fly man's contemptuous name for him. Along comes (we are ascending, rung by rung, that social ladder, reader) a man who fishes with flies, but with streamer flies, which imitate not insects but minnows. Big fish feed on minnows, and so this fisherman also has filled his creel. Along comes a wet-fly fisherman; wet flies imitate insects but are fished underwater. This fisherman, too, has fish, for a statistical reason presently to be explained. With differing degrees of intolerance, the dry-fly man looks down upon them all. For him, in the words of an old song, it ain't what you do, it's the way what you do it. His creel may be empty (he may not even carry a creel; he may belong to that most select group of all: those who would never dream of killing a trout, who put back all they catch) yet he will not switch, though he knows as well as any of them, indeed, better than any of them, that big fish, the kind he too is after, seldom stir themselves for a morsel of food that would require a diamond merchant's scale to register its microscopic weight, and he knows that all trout, even little ones, take only about ten percent of their food on the surface of the water, where he is fishing. And the strange part is, that though they regard him as daft, and subject him to much joking, down deep those other varieties of fishermen have a sneaking admiration for his quixotry, and yield him without grudge his place at the top of the ladder.

6

MEASURING YOUR FISH BEFORE YOU catch him is counting your chickens before they hatch; but as I did not much expect to catch that big one-eyed trout, I measured him first. It was possible to do this because he always lay at his feeding station with his blind side almost touching the bank. I went to the pool at break of day the morning after discovering him, carrying with me a carpenter's six-foot folding rule. I stretched it, and myself, upon the bank. In addition to the rule, I took with me my wife, and while I do not expect to be believed myself, I trust that no one is unchivalrous enough to doubt her word. She too was stretched upon the bank, and she is ready to affirm that the fish measured forty-two and a fraction inches. I did not attempt to tape-measure his girth, but I have

43

measured that of my own thigh, to which it corresponded. When the length and the girth of a fish are known, its weight can be roughly estimated. I estimated old One-eye's to be thirty pounds, give or take five.

He could never have attained that prodigious size in that little pool. He must have come down, and not very long before, from Stockbridge Bowl, perhaps been washed down in a flood. Nor could he have attained that size half-blind. The loss of that eye, too, had to be fairly recent. Nor could he have attained that size on a diet limited to the tiny insects that he was now daintily feeding on.

But this was a very old fish, and old fish, like old people, experience a decline of appetite, and old trout do not like to exert themselves. Tables have been worked out showing how many calories, or fractions thereof, there are in a may fly and how many ergs of energy a trout of a certain weight must expend per foot of movement in water with a current of a certain force, and what it all adds up to is: the more a big fish eats the more it starves. Old One-eye had once been even bigger than he was.

Now, a fish that big cannot be caught. That he has not been is all the proof needed that he cannot be. He is too wise. He never got that big without being wise. The allotted life-span of the trout—which only the tiniest fraction of them attain—is seven years, by which age the average one is twenty-two inches long. Cyclops was just under double that—had he likewise doubled the normal life-span? Was he, in age, the equivalent of a human being of 140? He must in his time have seen— and seen through—all the 3,000 patterns of artificial flies that are said to exist. Considering the odds against it, his survival to that age made him a Hercules, a Solomon, a Tithonus of trout.

On the other hand, a fish that big is too big not to be fished for.

What happens is that the fish hooks the fisherman.

I struggled hard to get free of that one. I knew he could not be caught, even handicapped as he was by being half-blind. That would only make him all the warier. He could not be caught—certainly not in the only way worthy of him, the way in which I was obliged to fish for him, with a floating fly. Certainly not by me. I knew I was no match for that fish, very possibly the record American trout.

I considered sending this letter:

Mr. Lee Wulff

Dear Sir:

In return for a season's private tuition in fly fishing from you, I will guide you to the biggest living brown trout.

I enjoyed the thought of Lee Wulff's rushing out and chartering a pontoon plane for us.

That would have been the fitting thing to do: to have given that fish to the man who was his match. That would have been the sporting thing to do. It would, and I knew this at the time, have been the prudent thing to do.

I knew how dangerous a sport fly fishing for trout can be. I have since come to know personally some of its casualties—and to shudder. I speak not of the phys-

45

ical dangers—though every sufficiently old fishing club has on its wall one or more coiled leaders with a fly attached and a label that reads, "Tom Smith's last cast," meaning the one he had on when they found him and fished him out, drowned while wading, or the victim of heart stoppage, possibly brought on by excitement over the biggest fish of his life. Such cases, however, are comparatively uncommon; the danger I refer to is more widespread, and more insidious. It is mental, emotional. Fly fishing for trout has wrecked men's marriages, their careers; when begun early enough in life it has prevented them from ever getting around to either marriage or a career and turned them into lifelong celibates and ne'er-do-wells. I have known some. Two whom I know had the strength of will to cure themselves of chronic alcoholism, but not of their addiction to fly fishing. Theodore Gordon threw up his job at an early age, sponged off his relatives, remained a lifelong bachelor, neglected his old, dying mother, and did nothing but two things with himself: fish for trout and, out of season, tie flies to fish through the coming one. There are, incidentally, a great many fishermen who think his was an exemplary life. The danger of becoming that kind of addict not only scared me, it appalled me. Before all excess the healthy, well-balanced mind draws back in distaste and fright; such zeal for a mere sport is particularly unbecoming. I both pity and despise any person who makes a passion out of a pastime. I know that, like everything else, moderation can be carried to excess; nonetheless, I am a firm believer in moderation.

That is my belief—in practice I am excessive in everything I do, and I had long suspected that my failure to master fly fishing had been a blessing in disguise, like the man prevented from becoming a lush because he could never hold down the stuff. Now providence had placed in my path a fish that was enough to unbalance a stabler man than I, and had restricted my method of angling for him by putting those boys there, committing a crime against nature that nothing less than the purest and most high-minded method, one I had tried, failed at and forsworn, could make up for. I wanted that fish and I wished I had never laid eyes on him. I had not lost a leg to him, but he had certainly taken a big bite of my brain.

I EQUIPPED MYSELF WITH THE FINEST
TACKLE. The fish deserved no less. I deserved a
great deal less, and that was why I bought the best:
I needed all the help I could get. To obtain it I went
to New York City, there being no tackle shops anywhere in my area for the very good reason that there
was no fishing, the only sizeable river being a sewer.
My purchases made the shopowner friendly—
inquisitive he was by nature. My accent betrayed me
and I owned up to being from Texas. On my way to
Canada to do some fishing. Little celebration for bringing in another gusher.

I needed instruction, but I had no one to instruct
me. In those days there were none of the fly-fishing
schools of which there is such a proliferation nowadays. If there had been, I would have gone and

enrolled under an alias and giving a false address, and in just three days—at least, so they promise in their ads—even I would have graduated a bachelor in the art and the science, and come back and laid educated siege to old Cyclops.

I had never known a fly fisherman. Since my ignominious failure to make one of myself and my retrogression to worms, I had not wanted to know one. I had avoided any closer contact with the few I saw at a distance on streams from time to time. But even if I had known one, known him well, I would not have trusted myself to seek his help now. Indeed, I would have shunned him altogether. He would surely have noticed my state of excitement. His curiosity would have been piqued. My eagerness, my impatience to learn, and to put my knowledge to work, would have given me away. A wild look, that of one who has gazed on wonders, haunted my eyes in those days. Fly fishermen are a suspicious crew, and their suspicions run on one thing. My secret would have been guessed, and I would have been shadowed to its source in Shadow Brook.

I sought instruction in books—no other sport has spawned so many. The literature of angling falls into two genres: the instructional and the devotional. The former is written by fishermen who write, the latter by writers who fish. I had read extensively in piscatorial prose of the devotional sort, searching always for the works of literature that some critics said were to be found there. I found one—if, that is to say, *Moby Dick* is a fish story. I turned now to the manuals.

From the furtiveness of my manner in asking for a book on the subject anybody would have thought it was

on how to do *It*. The salesclerk—one of those unfor-
tunates whose dreaminess declared better than a blood
test that he too had been bitten by the tsetse fly of trout
fishing and would never amount to anything—guided
me to volumes that he said were "the latest thing." That
drew me up. Innocent that I was, I supposed that one
manual on fly fishing, updated periodically to include
new tackle, would suffice for all time, the same as one
on sex. That the sport had had a long continuity, I
knew; but I supposed it just flowed quietly in the same
old channel down to the same old sea, that its tenets
had been laid down in one bible a long time ago and
gone unrevised ever since. I learned now that it had a
history, and that history was rife with revolutions and
upheavals, especially, as might be expected, in these
turbulent and changeful modern times. Fishing had
indeed had its Age of Faith, its long, slumbrous, unre-
formated Dark Ages; but the era of inquiry and
technology had affected it as it had all else. The days of
fishing as an inexact art and a thoughtless pastime
belonged to—only so archaic a *mot* is *juste*—
yesteryear. If you were to compete with the crowds
now on the streams in quest of trout you needed to be a
physicist, an entomologist, a limnologist, a statistician,
a biometrician. The angler had metamorphosed into
the ichthyologist, and the prevailing prose reflected
the change—if mud can be said to reflect. I found
myself correcting it as I had done freshman themes in
my years as a professor. You had to hack your way
through it as through a thicket. Participles dangled,
person and number got separated and lost, clichés
were rank, thesaurusitis and sesquipedalianism ran
rampant, and the rare unsplit infinitive seemed out of

place, a rose among nettles. Yet, instead of weeding their gardens, these writers endeavored to grow exotics in them: orchids, passionflowers Inside each of them was imprisoned a poet, like the prince inside the toad. What came out was a richness of embarrassments: shoddy prose patched with purple — beautifully written without first being well written.

To solve that most basic of problems, which artificial fly to offer the fish, one of my authorities, the one I called The Efficiency Expert, counseled approaching the stream with a net, a bottle of formaldehyde, and the highest power microscope you could conveniently carry. Plant your net in the stream like a seine stretching from bank to bank, go upstream and turn over some rocks on the creekbed, go back to your net, pick off the little nymphs that have washed down against it, get out your microscope and identify them, then with your handy streamside fly-tying kit containing an assortment of hooks in twenty different sizes, tinsels, threads of all colors, feathers and furs from all the world's feather- and fur-bearers, tie artificials to match — or to match not those nymphs, if you were a dry-fly purist, like me, but the winged adults of which those were the nymphs. This same expert had done field studies and had counted and worked out the number of casts made by the average angler in an average day on the water. It came to 8,500. As his own approach, with its extended foreplay, left him time to make far fewer than that, he was concerned that every one of his should count. His goal — unattainable — was that his every cast should be without drag, that deadliest of all the fly fisherman's many, many enemies, for when the fly drags on the water the fish not only smells a rat and refuses the fly, he refuses every fly for the next twenty-four hours, more or less, because it scares the living daylights out of him. Using this dodge and that, The Efficiency Expert had worked out ways to avoid drag that resulted in adding as much as a week to the fishing season, practically speaking. Ah, yes, I thought, we could all of us use a little more of that drag-free float, in every walk of life, in every endeavor. And I thought, "Oh, Cyclops! Into what deep and murky waters you have led me!"

From The Entomologist I learned that when the fish are being finicky—"selective" is the word—about the fly they are feeding on, the angler must match it. When, for example, it is *Ephemerella subvaria* that they are all eating like peanuts, then you must show them the Hendrickson fly, not the Quill Gordon, which was all they would look at last week when *Iron fraudator* was in season. A glimmer of hope in a fog of confusion: every species of aquatic insect has its hatching time fixed as surely as it takes you nine months to ripen; ready or not, it can no longer stay in its protective pupa, snug in the silt of the creekbed, past a certain hour of a certain date: willy-nilly, it must emerge into this cruel world of waiting and voracious trout. So it would seem that the angler could get away with something like, "If this is Tuesday then it must be Blue-winged Olive." Alas, there are, for trout, more different *plats-de-jour* than there are days of your years. There are, in the streams of North America, as many different kinds of aquatic insects as there are stars in the Milky Way. To be sure, not all of these are staples of

trout diet, and thus essential for the angler to know—
only some 1,500, with a few thousand variations as to
size.

When I read the learned entomologist;
When the proofs, the figures, were ranged in columns
*   before me;*
When I was shown the charts and diagrams, to add,
*   divide, and measure them;*
When I, sitting, read the entomologist
How soon, unaccountable, I became tired and sick;

and this vision of myself came to me: I stood waist-
deep in my waders in a heavy current with a swarm
around my head of some 1,500 insects, each infinites-
imally different, and *I was able to identify each and every
one of them!*

"*Heptagenia elegantula,*" I intoned. "*Ephemerella infre-
quens. Cinygmula ramaleyi. Rhithrogena impersonata. Siph-
lonurus quebecensis. Paraleptophlebia adoptiva. Epeorus
pleuralis . . .*"

It was the learned but mindless mumble of the
idiot-savant. I closed that volume as though slamming
down the lid on Pandora's box. Demented I might be,
but that way lay madness maddened.

I, sitting, read the learned entomologist;
Till rising and gliding out, I wandered off by myself,
In the mystical moist night air, and from time to time,
Swatted in perfect ignorance at the bugs.

8

IT WAS I, ALONE, UNAIDED, WHO SOLVED
my problem. I hit upon a solution which, though I
say so myself, was brilliant. Crafty. Sly. Stunning-
ly original. It was elementary, of course; every
brilliant stroke is—after somebody has had it! Like so
many advances, mine consisted in going at things
backward. The problem: I needed a mentor. The pre-
dicament: I knew no one, could trust no one. As long as
I kept thinking of my preceptor as a fisherman, I got
nowhere. Once I thought of him as a fish—eureka!
Who knew more about the ways of trout than the
world's greatest trout, one of the all-time greats? Here
I had him in a fishbowl of a pool, and he was blind on
one side; without his seeing me, I could study his every
move, every mood.

I went to the pool. I set out in plainclothes, taking no

tackle with me. For a long time to come I would have no need of any. Then, suddenly seeing myself as others might see me, a man out at odd, twilight hours, stealthy, furtive, up to something or other, I reconsidered and went disguised with gear. When I got there I found those wicked boys up to their tricks.

I had forgotten about them. In my mind that fish had grown even greater than he was, and I had grown a great deal greater than I was, and in my mental photograph of the two of us, me smiling modestly as I held him up by his tail, those boys with their despicable tactics had been crowded completely out of the picture. Now there they were, one of them yanking a bluegill onto the bank, another stepping on his fish, still another with his bloody little paws busy at their grisly task. A fit resembling in all its symptoms an apoplectic stroke seized me. A superstitious dread, which turned instantly into a dead certainty, gripped me. I was convinced on the spot that those little Yankees, natives of the place, unlike me, knew something I did not know: that for a resentful old one-eyed cannibal trout, fishes' eyes were a sure-fire bait, that generations of Berkshire Mountain boys had known this; and so real that I all but saw it transpiring before my eyes was this sickening vision: one of those cane poles bent double, a shout of, "I got him!" raised in a boyish soprano, and my fish, my trophy fish, was ingloriously hauled ashore by that whole brood of little imps.

As soon as I showed up, of course, they skulked away. And they made themselves scarce for however long I stood guard, defending One-eye against them and against his own savage proclivities. But I could not be there around the clock, not without neglecting both work and wife. Just the mornings, the afternoons and the evenings until boys' bedtimes.

It was a change of season, bringing with it an annual American rite, that delivered me from the threat they posed. One day as I came on my afternoon shift, one sunny, shirtsleeve, get-out-of-doors day, I passed the Interlaken playground and there they all were. The cry of "Batter up!" piped in clear, sweet, childish tones, trilled like birdsong upon the vernal air. Baseball season had come to the Berkshires—late, like all seasons, except winter. Blessings upon those Little Leaguers and might they one and all grow up to be a second Babe Ruth! A small and rather dingy but nonetheless inspiriting copy of Old Glory fluttered on its staff above this enactment of The National Pastime. Proceeding on my way to the pool, my pool, I dilated with devotion toward this sports-conscious country of ours. I not only blessed baseball, I was grateful for golf, thankful for tennis, ecstatic for aquatics—for all those many health-giving, body- and character-building warm-weather pursuits that keep our people in tone, and out of trout streams.

9

M Y TIME TO LEARN FROM OLD ONE-eye was short—what was left of this season. Neither he nor I would be here next year. I would be gone from the country; he would surely be dead. He was too old to survive another Berkshire winter. He could not live long in this little pool. No scope for his bulk here. He was home from sea, passing his decline in this sailors' snug harbor.

Each day that I went there to learn from him how to kill him, I waited anxiously for his appearance and rejoiced to find that he was still alive. I was not fearful that some other of his natural enemies might have gotten in ahead of me and killed him overnight. None had up to now; he had outsmarted, outfought them all. I feared only that he might have cheated me by dying a natural death. He was now fighting his first losing battle, the one against the common enemy of fish and men.

I logged his comings and goings like an assassin establishing his victim's routine. He came always to the same feeding station, an eddy at the tail of the pool where a tiny feeder stream trickled in, like an old regular of a restaurant to the table reserved for him. If there were other trout in the pool, none dared appropriate his place. When I had fixed the hours at which he issued from his lair beneath the bridge, then I was there, prone on the bank beside his spot, waiting for him to come to breakfast at dawn, to dinner at dusk. He was unfailingly punctual in keeping the appointment with me that he never knew he had. Almost cheek to cheek with his sworn enemy he lay. And though he was a prodigy of his kind and I merely representative of mine, yet nature had given to me a dubious superiority which made me pity him: unlike me, he did not know that he must die.

But though he might be ignorant of the end awaiting him, the fish acted as though he felt himself threatened every moment of his existence. Such a jittery creature he was, ever alert, ever fearful, as though he understood that he lived his life in a medium that exposed to hostile view his every movement. The fleeting shadow of a cloud passing over him was enough to send him darting for safety underneath the bridge. Old and big and wise in his way as he was, he could never for an instant relax his lifelong vigil; indeed, he must redouble it, for now he had but one eye with which to be twice as watchful.

That blind eye put between him and me the equivalent of a one-way mirror, and, lying motionless in shallow, still, clear water, he could be observed as though he were in a tank in a laboratory, or in a home aquarium. Yet, long as I studied him, and at such close range, I never got accustomed to him, never quite believed in his actuality. His difference from all others of his kind was too gross, too offensive to the established order of things. Surely for the latter part of his life his very size must, paradoxically, have been a protection against man, a conspicuous cover, if you will, a kind of flagrant camouflage. He was simply too big to be believed. Not looking for a trout his size, fishermen did not see him, or if one did, he disbelieved his own eyes, dismissed the apparition as a figment of his fevered imagination, a fisherman's fantasy, and, knowing well how fishermen's tales are received by the world, never told a living soul. Thus, unseen, or else rejected as an impossibility and cloaked in universal silence, a wonder unrenowned, the fish had grown bigger and bigger.

It might be expected that such a monster, such a freak, would be clumsy, musclebound, weak, short of wind, but the fish's great bulk was no impediment to his grace, his agility, his might. From dead still, he could, when alarmed, accelerate to his full power with a speed that amounted to vanishing on the spot—a magician's trick: now you see it, now you don't. Every part of that bullet of a body of his was functional. His mastery of his element was total. Without the movement of a muscle he could maintain himself as stationary as a stone. By inflating and deflating his air-bladder, he surfaced and sounded like a submarine, and just as stealthily. He would sight his prey as it entered the pool. Then, light as a bubble he rose, his dorsal fin broke water like a periscope, his huge streamlined snout silently dimpled the surface, and into that great maw of his a grasshopper or a caterpillar or a late-hatching may fly drifted, borne helplessly on the current. Mission accomplished, he sank soundlessly from sight. When he wriggled to propel himself forward, the undulation of his muscles caused his spots to ripple like those on the side of a dappled horse when it quivers to the bite of a fly.

Meanwhile, my studies were not confined to the fish, his hours, his preferences in food—which were, in any case, whimsical and unpredictable in ways which the books scanted. It was equally important that I familiarize myself with his immediate surroundings, that small dining area of the pool in which, if at all, he was to be taken unawares. I had to chart the currents I would be fishing as carefully as a riverboat pilot. That my river—the little feeder stream that served up the fish's food to him—was no more than two feet wide and not much longer than that before it was dissolved into the pool itself, that it was slow and unruffled, and that my fly would float on its surface, above any obstructions, might seem to make my task easy. Not so. The very narrowness of the channel would demand a cast of pinpoint accuracy, the very shortness of it would mean that my time of drag-free float would be fractions of a second, and the very stillness of the surface meant that my fly must fall upon it so unnoticeably as to seem not to have fallen but to have hatched from under it.

And even then there was still another worry.

There was—there always is, in even the narrowest stretch of flowing water—though barely discernible, more currents than one. This is what, sooner or later, always causes drag, that oft-mentioned enemy of the dry-fly fisherman. The fisherman's fly must ride down the current that ensnares the live insects and carries them to the lurking fish. Meanwhile, the leader to which the fly is attached lies across the adjacent current, or currents. No two currents of a stream, however small, however slow, however close the two, flow at the same speed. One of them will carry the leader downstream at a rate faster than that of the fly. After a while—about as long as it takes to read this—the leader bellies in the current downstream of the fly and begins to drag the fly faster and faster as it lengthens. Nothing could be more unlike the free float of the natural insect, and trout are all born knowing this. Furthermore, they not only refuse that one unnatural fly—so unsettling is the sight, they quit feeding altogether and hide themselves in fright. The fisherman's time in which to deceive and hook the fish is that brief interval between the alighting of his fly upon the water and the commencement of drag. Drag a fly over a wise, wary old trout, and you had might as well move on.

I would have yet another problem. The limitation of the fish's vision, which had worked to my advantage while I studied him, would be a disadvantage when I came to fish for him. The field of view of a normal trout is just ninety-seven and six-tenths degrees. Within that narrow compass the fisherman's fly must be presented; if the fish is to take it, he must see it. Only half that would I have in which to attract, entice, and deceive old One-eye. To put down a fly, from a distance of some forty feet, on that small a target would be about like asking a bombardier to hit a one-lane bridge from five miles' altitude, and, if it was not to frighten the fish away, the fly must alight with the delicacy of a wisp of down.

It was not that familiarity had bred contempt for him in me—if anything, my awe of him and my awareness of my problems had mounted to the point that I was almost paralyzed by them—that made me decide the time had come to take him on. I had just wakened to the realization that it was August—late August, almost September. The year's first yellow leaf falling to the water before me was what wakened me. The fishing season was fast running out. That wizard of a fish had cast his spell over me. Another of his protective devices; by his very fascination he could beguile you into forgetting your intentions toward him.

There is a way to land a really big fish—maybe. It is the opposite of the way to land an ordinary one. Instead of fighting him, you put no pressure on him at all; indeed, you do not let him know that he is hooked. You give him his head. You just hold on quietly and let him have the freedom of the pool, until the moment when you scoop him up tail-first in your net. That was what the fish had done to me. Without my even knowing I was hooked, he had had me all but ready for the net. Now or never, I must get up off my belly and into the water with him.

I then learned that we were not alone, my fish and I. While I had been observing him on that day of decision, I was being observed myself.

10

AFTER THAT BIG OLD TROUT?"

I was crawling backward away from the bank. Looking over my shoulder, I saw a towheaded little boy, as freckled as a trout. I spent another minute on my hands and knees searching for the thing I was pretending to have lost.

"After that big old trout, eh?"

"Trout?" I inquired, giving up my search and getting to my feet. "What trout?"

The boy stepped around me and started down the path to have a look for himself. He knew where to look.

"Don't go too near!" I said. "You'll scare him."

"Scare him? What's he got to be scared of? Hell, he's bigger'n I am."

"Well then, keep back. If you should slip and fall in, he might eat you."

73

"You a foreigner?"

"Texan."

"Thought you talked kind of funny. Well, let me tell you something, Tex. You're wasting your time fishing for that big old one-eyed trout."

"Done a good bit of fishing yourself, have you?"

"Enough to know that. I'm just telling you for your own good."

"Son, if I'd always done what was good for me I would never have had much fun."

The boy watched as I rigged my rod. From a pocket of my vest I took one of my many fly boxes and selected a fly.

"What's that?" the boy asked.

I showed him the Hairwing Coachman, size 10, that I had chosen.

"What is it?" he asked.

"An artificial fly. A hook with feathers tied around it to look like a live insect." Actually, the Hairwing Coachman imitates no known insect. It's the fly for entomological ignoramuses, like me.

"What's it for?"

"It's my bait."

"That? You think you're going to catch that fish with that thing?" The boy pitied me. To him my foolishness was monumental. "Mister," he said, "there's just one bait you might get that fish there to bite. Know what it is?"

"I suspect I know what you think it is," I said.

"It's—"

"Never mind."

"It's—"

74

"Never mind! You do things your way, I'll do them mine."

"You want to catch that fish, don't you? Well—"

"I do, but that's not all I want. There's more to fishing than catching fish."

With a shrug and a shake of his head, the boy gave up on me. He had done his best.

I went up over the bridge and around to the other side of the pool. I waded into the water behind the fish. I dared approach him no nearer than thirty-five feet. I flicked my line back and forth in false casts, adding to its length. When I judged it to be the proper length, I straightened it forward and let it drop. It touched water just where I wanted it to, and, so it seemed to me, touched softly. Nevertheless, the fish bolted for the bridge, much to the enjoyment of the boy on the bank.

11

WHAT I HAD DONE WAS DISREGARD the first and most famous dictum of fly fishing, that of the earliest writer on the subject, Walton's friend and companion, Charles Cotton: "Fish fine and far off."

In fly fishing, the lure—the artificial fly itself—being weightless, it is the weight of the line that the fisherman casts. This makes it far too heavy and conspicuous a thing to fool even the most foolish fish, and among trout of any size there are few foolish ones. To get "fine and far off" the fisherman is forced to interpose between the line and the fly an additional piece of tackle, one which, in the already unequal contest between him and the fish, gives the decisive advantage to the fish. It is, of course, the fish that dictates—one might say, designs—every piece of the fisherman's tackle, but with this one he practically assures an out-come favorable to himself. This is the leader, the trans-lucent terminal addition to the fisherman's line to which is attached the fly.

Nowadays leaders are made of nylon monofilament, but traditionally they were made of something that perhaps gives a better idea of their gossamer nature: the drawn and finely stretched gut of silkworms.

A leader's diameter is measured with a micrometer, in thousandths of an inch. It tapers from butt to tippet, going from about the size of carpet thread down to something that looks as though it were spun by an anemic spider. In fishing for trout, a leader nine feet long is the shortest ever used; anything less than that puts the heavy and highly visible line—or its equally alarming shadow—too near the fish. The maximum length? There is none. It is whatever the fish demands, and the fisherman can cast—for the longer the leader the harder it is to handle. In broken water, early-season, deep, fast, turbid water, and with small, un-sophisticated fish, one can get away with a shorter and coarser leader; later in the season, with the water low, slow-moving, and clear, and always with big, wise, wary old fish, the leader grows ever longer, ever finer, with the fisherman further handicapping himself with each foot he adds to the tippet, hoping to stop at the point where the leader is fine enough to fool the fish but still strong enough to hold and land him.

Now, when I say "big, wise and wary trout," it should be understood that I am talking about those of three pounds and over. Even the skilled and dedicated fisherman catches very few that big; rare is the man who has taken a single fish of four pounds or over in a lifetime. In the eastern United States nowadays a two-pound trout is a big one. My Cyclops was fifteen times that size and surely to the fifteenth power wiser, warier. Thus, paradoxically, the biggest of fish was to push me to use the lightest of leaders. Our campaign against each other was fought over thousandths of an inch, with me yielding steadily to him.

With each concession I made to him I came nearer to enticing, deceiving, and hooking him and further from ever landing him if I should. I had begun with a nine-foot leader terminating in a tippet of .011 inch diameter with a dead-weight breaking strength of nine pounds. This the fish not only disdained, he let me know it was a gross insult to his intelligence and unworthy even of mine.

As, over the succeeding weeks, I grudgingly added length to, and subtracted strength from my leader—and as I learned to cast the clumsy thing (which took a great deal longer to do than it does to tell)—I had the satisfaction, and the anxiety, of seeing a growing change in the response of my adversary.

THE BOSTON SYMPHONY ORCHESTRA WAS IN its summer home and the concert season on up at Tanglewood, drawing music-lovers from all over the northeast. On Sundays a steady stream of cars passed over the bridge in Interlaken—over me—on their way there, then when the concert ended, came down in a stampede. On one rather somber Sunday, when the people of the settlement were all shut indoors and when the low cover of clouds put a lid on things and sounds carried far and wide, down from above came the distant thunder of Beethoven's "Ode to Joy." The music seemed to be coming from light-years off, and so vast was the number of voices in the choir that had been assembled, it sounded like the hosts of heaven: ethereal harmony, music of the spheres.

Conscious that my time was short, I applied myself closely, and under the fish's strict tutelage I was becoming a better fisherman. He demanded nothing less than perfection. A careless cast, one that missed its aim by an inch or that landed with the least disturbance, and he was gone. Such ineptness seemed not so much to frighten as to affront him. He then retired beneath the bridge as though to allow me to beat an unwatched retreat. How fatuous of me it seemed then ever to have thought I was going to catch that wonder of the world. In this feeling I was unfailingly seconded by my companion, the towheaded, frecklefaced little boy on the bank.

Until, that is, he gave me up as a hopeless case, lost interest, and no longer appeared at the pool. The appeal of fishing as a spectator sport is limited at best; with never a nibble, I provided no excitement whatever, only the laughable spectacle of a wrongheaded and stubborn fool, deaf not just to local wisdom but to plain common sense. I was relieved to be rid of him.

I was improving steadily, and all the same I remained as far short as ever of the mastery, the magic, needed to entice this phenomenon of a fish into taking my fly. The longer I fished for him and the better I got at it, the more elusive he seemed to grow, as though he were leading me—as he alone among trout could do—into the most rarefied realms of trout fishing. I got good enough, or so I felt, to be justified in wondering whether there was a man alive who could catch this fish.

Steadily forcing me to yield to him in the battle of the lengthening leader, he now had me down to one eighteen feet long, spidery thin. With that I could see I was beginning to interest him. So big was he that even at my distance from him I could detect that rippling of his spots which denoted that he was tensing, readying himself to pounce upon his approaching prey. He looked then like a jet plane throbbing as its engines are revved up for the take-off. I too throbbed with tension at those times. He would raise himself, wait, watch. Then at the last moment he always had second thoughts, sank back and let my fly drift past. I had said it to myself before, I now became convinced that this fish had attained his extraordinary size, his uncommon age, thanks to some faculty that made him unique among his kind, perhaps in the history of his kind. I alternated between cursing him for his invulnerability and feeling that I had been uniquely privileged to have made the acquaintance of so remarkable, so rare a creature.

I grew increasingly conscious of my debt to him, yet I remained ungrateful. He was giving me incomparable training in how to catch trout—lesser trout than himself, that is, and that included them all. He was testing me against the highest possible standards. Few fishermen had ever had such coaching as his of me. I should have been content with that. I was not. He himself was the fish I wanted to catch, I hardly cared whether I ever caught another, and, forgetting now that I owed my betterment all to him, in my increasing pride and vainglory I grew more and more confident that I could, that I would. Right up to the season's closing day I continued to believe that.

"CLOSING DAY," MY SMALL COMPANION met me with at poolside.

"Has come. Aye, Caesar. But not gone," I rejoined.

"Huh?" My talking in riddles was all that was needed to convince him that I was hopelessly addled.

"Still using them artificial flies, I see."

"Mmh."

"Ever get him to bite one of them yet?"

"Can't say I have."

"Then what makes you think he's going to now at the last minute?"

"Don't think he's going to—just hoping he might. You never know when your luck will change."

But the truth was, the boy had dashed my hopes. Closing day it was, and that alone would be the thing to make this one different from all the other days I had sunk in this folly of mine. At midnight tonight the Fish and Game Commission of the Commonwealth of Massachusetts would extend legal protection over its most venerable trout, and he would live out his pensionage in this little pool. It was only out of a sense of obligation and to round out the fitness of things that I waded into the water. A sense that, having challenged the fish, I owed him his total triumph over me. It was I who had made today's appointment with him, and there he was.

As often happens, now that I had lost confidence, and, with it, the compulsion to perform, I exceled myself in my casting that day. Four times running I placed my fly—a No. 12 Black Gnat it was, to match the ones that were biting me—over the fish without rousing his suspicions, putting him off his feed and sending him to sulk beneath the bridge. Those repeatedly ignored casts made my young companion smirk; I, though rather ruefully, admired my unproductive accomplishment.

My fifth cast would have alighted in the same spot, some four feet in front of the fish, as the others had. However, it never did. Exploding from the water, the fish took it on the wing, a foot above the surface. Why that cast and none of the countless others, nobody will ever know. Instantly he felt the barb. Not fright, but fight, was what it brought out in him.

Out of the water he rose again like a rocket—out and out, and still there was more to him, no end to him. More bird than fish he seemed as he hovered above the water, his spots and spangles patterned like plumage. I half expected to see his sides unfold and spread in flight, as though, like the insects he fed upon, he had undergone metamorphosis and hatched. His gleaming wetness gave an iridescent glaze to him, and as he rose into the sunshine his multitudinous markings sparkled as though he were studded with jewels. At once weighty and weightless, he rose to twice his own length. Then, giving himself a flip like a pole-vaulter's, down he dove, parting the water with a wallop that rocked the pool to its edges.

The next moment I was facing in another direction, turned by the tug of my rod, which I was surprised to find in my hand. Nothing remotely resembling his speed and power had I ever experienced in my fishing. Nothing I might have done could have contained him. It was only the confines of the pool that turned him.

Straight up from the water he rose again. Higher than before he rose. It was not desperation that drove him. There was exuberance in his leap, joy of battle, complete self-confidence, glory in his own singularity. Polished silver encrusted with jewels of all colors he was, and of a size not to be believed even by one who had studied him for weeks. I believed now that he had taken my fly for the fun of it. I was quite ready to credit that superfish with knowing this was the last day of the season, even with knowing it was his last season, and of wanting to show the world what, despite age and impairment, he was capable of. Reaching the peak of his leap, he gave a thrash, scattering spray around him. In the sunshine the drops sparkled like his own spots. It was as though a rocket had burst, showering its scintillations upon the air.

Another unrestrainable run, then again he leaped, and for this one the former two had been only warmups. Surely he must have a drop of salmon in his blood! Up and up he went until he had risen into the bright sunshine, and there, in defiance of gravity, in suspension of time, he hung. He shook himself down his entire length. The spray that scattered from him caught the light and became a perfect rainbow in miniature. Set in that aureole of his own colors that streamed in bands from him, he gave a final toss of his head, breaking my leader with insolent ease, did a flip, dove and re-entered the water with a splash that sent waves washing long afterward against my trembling and strengthless legs.

"Dummy!" cried the boy on the bank. "You had him and you let him get away!"

EPILOGUE

EVEN SO WORLDLY A MAN AS JON-
ATHAN Swift could write late in life, in a
letter to his friend Alexander Pope, "I re-
member when I was a little boy, I felt a great
fish at the end of my line, which I drew up almost to the
ground, but it dropped in, and the disappointment
vexes me to this day." Sick with disappointment at
losing my once-in-a-lifetime fish, I was sure I would
never get over it.

But now I wonder, would I really rather have that
fish, or a plaster replica of him, hanging on my wall
than to see him as I do in my memory, flaunting his
might and his majesty against that rainbow of his own
making? Many times, when I was low in spirits, I have
rerun that vivid footage photographed by my eyes and
printed upon my mind, and been cheered, been glad

that that was my last view of him. He is the one fish of my life that has not grown bigger in recollection, the one that needs no assistance from me.

Fishing stories always end with the fish getting away. Not this one. This, reader, has been the story of a fisherman who got away. For old One-eye made a changed man of me. No fish since him has ever been able to madden me again. I have hooked and lost some big ones in that time, but to each and all I have been able to say, "Go your way. I have known your better, known him well, and there will never be his like again. You, however big you may be, are a mere minnow compared to my Moby Dick."